사과나무의 사랑

THE LOVE OF AN APPLE TREE

서울문학 출판부

ALSO BY YOON-HO CHO

Meet Like Wildflowers (1985)

The Poet's Tree (1992)

You, the Suffering Brooder (1997)

The River Empties Its Heart (2006)

사과나무의 사랑

THE LOVE OF AN APPLE TREE

YOON-HO CHO
조윤호 시집

Translated into and from Korean by
Rachel S. Rhee, Irene Seonjoo Yoon,
Kyung-Nyun Kim Richards &
Steffen Francis Richards

레이첼 S. 리, 윤선주, 김경년,
스테픈 프란시스 리챠즈 번역

Cross-Cultural Communication
Merrick, New York
2014

Editor/Publisher: Stanley H. Barkan

Published by
Cross-Cultural Communications
239 Wynsum Avenue
Merrick, NY 11566-4725/USA
Tel: 516-868-5635 / Fax: 516-379-1901
E-mails: cccpoetry@aol.com / cccbarkan@optonline.net
www.cross-culturalcommunications.com

ISBN 978-0-89304-993-5

Library of Congress Control Number: 2013955651

Korean Bilingual Poetry Series #1
in cooperation with Korean Expatriate Literature

First printing of Bilingual Edition: January 2014

Printed by Seoul Munhak Corp.
404 Gongduk-dong, Mapo-gu
Poonglim Vip Suite #1210
Seoul, Korea
Tel: 02-070-8711-2638

나는 미국에 와서 새 집을 짓고 뜰에는 사과나무 두 그루를 심었다. 오랫동안 살지 않더라도 누군가 이사를 와서 사과나무에 달린 사과를 따 먹을 수 있다면 좋을 것 같은 생각이 들었던 것이다.

언젠가 어느 가을날 내가 이민 초기에 살던 미시간 주 디트로이트 근처에 갈 일이 있어서 가 보았다. 내 이웃에 사는 미국 친구들을 만나보러 가게 되었다. 내가 살던 그 집 넓은 뒤뜰에 내가 심어놓았던 사과나무를 보았다. 정말 나뭇가지가 휘어질 정도로 많은 사과가 달려 가을볕에 타고 있는 것을 보게 되었다. 그때의 그 기쁜 마음을 좀처럼 감출 수가 없다.

오늘 내가 써 놓은 시들도 마찬가지로 내가 심어놓았던 그 때의 그 사과나무와 조금도 다를 바가 없다는 생각이 든다. 사과나무의 가지가 휘어질 정도로 사과가 열리듯 내 시들도 많은 독자들이 읽게 되었으면 좋겠다.

어쨌든 내 시집을 미국출판사 '크로스 컬추럴 커뮤니케이션스사'에서 출판하게 도와준 이 회사 대표인 스탠리 발칸 시인에게 먼저 고개 숙여 감사를 드린다.

이번에 내 시집을 한영 이중 언어로 낼 수 있도록 영어로 번역해 주신 번역가 Rachel S. Rhee 시인과 윤선주 시인, 김경년 시인, 스테픈 프란시스 리챠즈 시인에게도 아울러 감사를 드린다.

특히 서평을 품위있게 써 주신 Peter Thabit Jones 시인과 Carolyn Mary Kleefeld 시인, 이형권 문학 평론가, 그리고 송기한 문학 평론가에게도 감사 드린다.

2014
미국 로스앤젤레스에서
—조윤호

After I came to America and built a new house, I planted two apple trees in the yard. Even though we didn't live there for very long, I thought it would be nice if someone else moved in and could eat the apples hanging on the tree.

One autumn day, I had the opportunity to return to Detroit, Michigan, where I had lived in my early immigrant years. I visited my American friends who had been my neighbors. I saw the apple trees I had planted in the wide backyard of my old house. I saw many apples ripening in the autumn sun, enough to bend the branches. I could not hide my joyful heart of that moment.

Today, I think the poems I wrote are no different from those apple trees I planted back then. Just as many apples formed to the point of bending the branches, I would like as many readers to read my poems.

At any rate, I bow my head in thanks first to poet and company representative Stanley Barkan who helped publish my poetry book through the US publisher Cross-Cultural Communications.

My thanks also to translators Rachel S. Rhee, Irene Seonjoo Yoon, Kyung-Nyun Kim Richards & Steffen Francis Richards who translated my poetry book into English so that it could be published in two languages.

I wish to express my appreciation especially to those who wrote gracious comments for my poems. They are the poets Peter Thabit Jones and Carolyn Mary Kleefeld and literary critics Hyung Kwon Lee and Kihan Song.

2014
Los Angeles, California
—Yoon-Ho Cho

|차 례|

CONTENTS

제 1부
Part One

사과나무

봄에 피었던 사과 꽃이
하얗게 지고 있지요.

이 세상에 단 한번
피었던 꽃을 떠나 보내고도
사과나무는 울지 않지요.

가을볕에 탄
붉은 사과를 맛있게 먹으면
알겠지요.

긴긴 여름 더위를 오래 참고
상처 난 마음을 말하지 않은 이유를
가을에는 알 것 같아요.

APPLE TREE

Open in the spring,
apple blossoms are falling white.

Never does the apple tree cry,
even when losing the petals
it had once possessed

I will come to know in due season,
when I eat the crimson fruit
tanned with autumn sunshine,

the reason why the apple tree
never told me the secrets
of its summer-long suffering,
its private wound.

Translated from the Korean by Irene S. Yoon

사랑은 모닥불

모닥불이 빨갛게 타오른다.
겨울밤—
세상이 추위에 얼어붙은 시간에

불꽃은 칼날의 혀같이
날름거리며
마음과 마음을 하나로 타올라

두 개의 장작은
서로 기대어
짐을 지우지 않는다.

오히려 서로의 무거운 짐
스스럼없이 태워
아름다운 사랑의 불꽃이 된다.

LOVE IS THE BONFIRE

The campfire burns scarlet
Winter night—
At a time when the world has frozen with cold,

Flames dart in and out
Like the tongue of a blade
And burn, unifying heart and heart,

Two logs
Mutually leaning
Without burdening the other.

Instead they freely burn
Each other's heavy burden
And become flames of beautiful love.

Translated from the Korean by Rachel S. Rhee

물처럼 가는 길

나는 물이 가는 길을 따라
먼 길을 떠납니다.

물은 숲을 지나 큰 바위를 만나면
살짝 피해서 옆길로 갑니다.

산 아래 물웅덩이는 깊고 맑아
지나가던 염소 한 마리가 목을 축입니다.

물은 낮은 곳으로 흘러가더니
강을 이루고 바다를 만듭니다.

나는 아무 말 하지 않는 물처럼 흘러흘러
그대에게로 갑니다.

PATH LIKE WATER

I leave on a long journey
Following the path of water.

When water passes a forest and meets a boulder,
It lightly detours to a side road.

The pool of water at the mountain's foot is so deep and clear
That a passing goat wets its throat.

Water flows down to a lower place,
Then forms rivers and creates seas.

Like wordless water,
I flow flow to you.

Translated from the Korean by Rachel S. Rhee

우리가 꽃이 되어 준다면

우리가 꽃이 되어 준다면
벌과 나비가 찾아 올 테지.

우리가 길이 되어 준다면
더 멀리 갈 수 있을 테지.

우리가 따뜻한 마음을 준다면
겨울눈이 와도 춥지 않을 테지.

우리가 함께 길을 간다면
외롭지도 않을 테지.

한 지붕 아래 둘이 하나 되어 준다면
우리는 행복할 테지.

IF WE BECAME FLOWERS

If we became flowers
Perhaps bees and butterflies would seek us.

If we became pathways
Perhaps we could travel farther.

If we gave warm hearts
Perhaps we would not be cold even in snow.

If we were to travel together
Perhaps we would not feel lonesome.

If two became one under one roof
Perhaps we would be happy.

Translated from the Korean by Rachel S. Rhee

작은 꿈

눈 내리는 날
자동차 바퀴가 헛돌아가는
그런 인생일지라도
울지 마세요.

오늘보다 나은 내일이 있잖아요.
온화한 봄날
생기 넘치는 대지 위에
웃고 있는 꽃을 바라보세요.

만일 작은 꿈이 없다면
부러진 새의 날개같이
찢어진 장미꽃같이
생각만 해도 비참하지요.

잠시 후면 우리는 떠나야 합니다.
작은 것에 만족하며
늘 기쁨을 가지세요.
어둠 속에 빛나는 작은 꿈이 있잖아요.

A SMALL DREAM

Even if it's a life in which
Automobile wheels rotate uselessly
On a snowy day
Please don't cry.

Isn't there a tomorrow that's better than today.
Gaze at the smiling flowers
In the earth overflowing with life
On a gentle spring day.

Suppose we didn't have a small dream
How pitiful even to consider
Like a bird with broken wings
Or a torn rosebud.

We need to leave in a while.
Be satisfied with the small things
And always search for happiness.
For don't we have a small dream glowing in the dark?

Translated from the Korean by Rachel S. Rhee

숲길에서

숲길에서 헤맨다 해도
길이 없는 것은 아니니
어딘가에 새 길이 있고
나는 희망을 잃지 않으리.

나뭇가지에 부딪치고
거미줄에 걸려 눈이 따갑다 해도
그것은 삶의 한 부분이니
나는 고개를 들고 하늘을 보리.

밤이 되면 주위가 어두워
앞길이 캄캄하다 해도
내 갈길 가르쳐 주는 별을 보며
나는 밤새워 꿈이나 꾼다.

AT THE FOREST ROAD

Even if I lose my way in the forest
Still I will not lose hope
Since it's not as if no road exists
And somewhere there's a new road.

Even if I bump against branches
And my eyes sting from a spider web
These are also part of life
So I shall hold up my head and look at the sky.

Even when night falls so my surroundings darken
And the road ahead is pitch black
I look at the stars that teach me the way to go
And stay up dreaming dreams all night long.

Translated from the Korean by Rachel S. Rhee

연꽃을 보면

살다보면
괴로운 일도 많고
외롭고 슬픈 일도 있지.

그럴 때는
연못가에 가서
연잎이 하는 것을 배워야해.

비가 오면
연잎은 속으로 고통이 스며들지 않게
방울방울 빗물의 흔적을 지워버리지.

햇살과 작은 바람에도
연잎은 흔들리지만
뿌리는 진흙탕에서 견디어 내고 있지.

연꽃이 그냥 피는 것은 아니지.
당신도 연잎처럼 할 수 있어.
방울방울 눈물을 지워봐.

WHEN I LOOK AT THE LOTUS

In life
There are many painful events
As well as lonely and sad events.

At those times
It's necessary to go to a lotus pond
To learn what the lotus leaf does.

When it rains
It erases traces of rain drop by drop
So that suffering will not seep inside.

Although the lotus leaf is shaken
By sunbeams and small breezes
Its roots persevere in the mud.

The lotus flower does not just happen to bloom.
You too can do it like the lotus leaf.
Try erasing your tears drop by drop.

Translated from the Korean by Rachel S. Rhee

낚시꾼의 마음

강가에서 한 낚시꾼이 서 있었다.
나는 20파운드가 넘는 여러 마리 베스(Bass)를
낚아 올렸다가 놓아주고
낚아 올렸다가 놓아주는 광경을 본다.

사람들이 낚시꾼에게 물었다.
"잡은 큰 물고기들을 잡았다가 왜 놓아주느냐?"
낚시꾼은 그냥 웃기만 하였다.

사람들은 더 알고 싶어 하였다.
"당신의 프라이팬이 작아서 그러느냐?"
낚시꾼은 이번에도 더 크게 웃기만 하였다.

HEART OF THE FISHERMAN

By the river, a fisherman is fishing.
I watch the sight of numerous 20-pound-plus bass
Being caught and then cast loose
Caught and then cast loose.

People ask the fisherman,
"Why do you release the large fish you've caught?"
The fisherman only laughs.

People become even more curious,
"Is it because your frying pan is too small?"
This time the fisherman laughs even harder.

Translated from the Korean by Rachel S. Rhee

자연

초록 잎사귀 몇 개
풀꽃의 맑은 웃음 몇 개
새의 울음소리 몇 개
내 가슴에 담아가리.

풀을 뜯는 사슴 한 마리
날아다니는 잠자리 한 마리
다람쥐 한 마리
내 가슴에 묻어가리.

겨울 들판처럼
고뇌하거나
외롭고 마음 아플 때
내 가슴에서 그것들을 꺼내보리.

NATURE

Several green leaves
several wildflower smiles
several cries from a bird
I shall hang on my heart.

One deer grazing
one dragonfly flying
one squirrel
I shall bury in my heart.

When, like a winter field, I suffer,
or feel loneliness and pain,
I shall take these things out
from my heart to look at them.

Translated from the Korean by Rachel S. Rhee

가을날

가을이 되니
바람은 장미꽃을 떨어뜨린다.

꽃잎이 진 자리마다
숨겨진 가시가 있음을 보여준다.

아무리 꽃이 아름다워도
함부로 만지지 말라는 듯

가시에 찔려
피 흘리는 아픔을 피하라는 듯

가을은 올해도
내게 선생이 되어 가르친다.

AUTUMN DAY

Now that it's autumn
The wind drops rose petals.

It reveals the existence of hidden thorns
In all the places where flower petals fell.

As if to say not to touch carelessly
No matter how beautiful the flower.

As if to say to avoid the pain of bleeding
After being pricked by a thorn.

This year, autumn again
Becomes my teacher and instructs me.

Translated from the Korean by Rachel S. Rhee

겨울새

사람은
눈에 불을 단 새.
밤에도 잠들지 않는.

겨울은 유난히 춥고
눈은 이불같이 쌓여가지만
새는 깨어 있어야 하네.
따뜻한 봄을 보기 위해서는.

차라리 망각이 나을지도 몰라.
꺼져가는 의식을 흔드는
겨울바람을 잊기 위해서는.

우리가 비참한 것은 하나.
먹이가 없어서가 아니라
보석같이 숨겨놓은
새의 따뜻한 심장이 없으니.

WINTER BIRD

A man is a bird
with fire in his eyes
who never sleeps even at night.

The winter is cold
and the snow accumulates
like a comforter
and yet, the bird should stay awake
to see the warm spring.

Perhaps amnesia may be better
to forget about the wintry wind
that shakes his dying consciousness.

We are miserable
not because we're running out of food,
but because we don't have the warm heart of a bird
that we should have kept like a gem stone.

Translated from the Korean by Irene S. Yoon

작은 기쁨

파도가 잠잠하기만을
기다릴 수 없듯이
인생의 비바람도 피할 수 없네.

광풍이 비를 동반하고
먹구름 낀 바다에서
배를 후려쳤네.

"나는 두려움 없어, 배가 두 동강이 난다해도"

광풍은 배를 쓰러뜨리려
산 같은 파도를 몰고 와
흔들고, 까불고 최악의 발악을 했네.
광풍은 배를 쓰러뜨릴 그럴 의사는 없었지만.

나는 다행히 죽지 않고
고통 뒤에 오는
작은 기쁨을 맛보았네.

A LITTLE PLEASURE

As we can't expect all the time
that the ocean waves stay calm,
so unavoidable is the tempest of life.

The raging wind
accompanied by the rain
smashed the boat
in the dark cloudy ocean.
"I am not afraid . . .
even if the boat may break into pieces."

The wind did all it could do
with the mountain-high waves.
It shook, abused the boat infernally
until it was brought down . . .
though it didn't really mean to bring it down.

Fortunately, I survived,
to taste the happiness
that comes after the suffering.

Translated from the Korean by Irene S. Yoon

부부

우리는
바퀴 하나씩을 가지고 와서
손수레를 만들었다.

그때 내 눈이 콩깍지가 씌었는지
당신의 바퀴가 내 것보다
더 크고 더 멀리 달려갈 듯 보였다.

눈이 온다고 미끄러질 것을 염려하고
비가 온다고 물웅덩이에 빠질 것을 걱정한다면
당신의 바퀴 하나 들고 조용히 떠나야 하리.

먼 길을 가려면
앞에서 끌고 뒤에서 밀며
한 방향으로 끝까지 달려가야 하리.

A COUPLE

We each
brought a wheel
to make a pushcart.

As if my eyes were covered with something
back then, yours appeared
larger and able to go farther
than mine.

Should you worry about slipping on snow
or falling into a puddle after rain,
you would better leave quietly.

To travel the long road,
we need to push and pull each other,
front and back,
running in one direction till the end.

Translated from the Korean by Irene S. Yoon

상처

꽃은 아름다워도
장미 가시는
하나의 작은 꽃 속에
깊이깊이
얼굴을 숨긴다.

한 번 찔리면
피 한 방울 흘리지 않아도
상처는 온갖 아픔을 불러들인다.

당신과 나 사이에도
깊이깊이
고통을 불러들인다.

WOUND

As in a beautiful blossom,
the thorn of a rose
deeply deeply
hides her face
in a small bud.

Once pricked,
even without a drop of blood,
injury becomes every possible pain.

Deeply deeply
brings in suffering
between you and me.

Translated from the Korean by Irene S. Yoon

거미

날마다
한 마리 거미의 꿈을 꾸네.

바람 불고
비 오는 날에도
외줄을 타다가 떨어지지 않을 거미.

거미가
그 작은 입술로
거미줄에 묻은 아침 이슬을 털고 있네.

새 세상을 향해
삶과 죽음의 외줄을 타고
건너야할 초점을 겨냥해

희망의 길 찾아 헤매는
거미의 꿈.

SPIDER

Everyday
I dream of a spider.

A spider that does not fall on its single thread
Even on rainy
And windy days.

The spider
Is shaking off the morning dew on the web
With that small mouth.

Towards a new world
Riding the thread of life and death
Aiming for the focal point it has to cross

Wandering, searching for the road of hope
The spider's dream.

Translated from the Korean by Rachel S. Rhee

석류

높은 나뭇가지에서
석류 한 알 떨어뜨린 것은
한 마리 갈까마귀.

나는 석류나무 밑을 지나다가
땅에 떨어져
빨간 빛깔의 석류를 바라보니

깨어진 석류는 반쯤 입을 벌린 채
마치 보석 같은 이빨로
웃고 있는 듯

새빨간 여인의 입술처럼
내 마음은 깨어진 석류 알로 물들어
하루 종일 웃었네.

POMEGRANATE

A raven
dropped a pomegranate
from a high branch.

When I looked at the red pomegranate
fallen on the ground,
while passing beneath a pomegranate tree,

the broken pomegranate
with its mouth half open,
as if laughing with jewel-like teeth,

my heart stained with broken pomegranate seeds
like a woman's red lips,
smiled all day long.

Translated from the Korean by Rachel S. Rhee

선인장을 보면

좋은 날씨,
아름다운 음악,
미소 짓는 얼굴,
이런 세상을 꿈꾸겠지요.

불볕 더위,
데스밸리 사막,
선인장 꽃,
이런 세상도 아름다울지 몰라요.

모래만이 가득한 이 땅에
소나기 한 번 내리기를 기다리며
모래를 씹고
밤마다 별을 보며
꽃을 피워낸 선인장을 보면

WHEN I SEE THE CACTUS

Good weather,
Beautiful music,
Smiling faces—
This may be the world of your dreams.

Scorching heat,
Desert of Death Valley,
Cactus flowers—
This kind of world may be beautiful, too.

When I see the cactus which has bloomed
While gazing at the stars each night,
Chewing sand,
And waiting for a sudden shower,
This land is filled only with sand.

Translated from the Korean by Rachel S. Rhee

가을밤의 산행

해가 저문 가을밤에
친구와 둘이서 산의 정상을 오른다.

구름이 가려 희미한 달빛은 무겁게 짓누른다.
나뭇가지에 팔과 다리, 얼굴이 스친다.

얼마쯤 올라갔을까?
내 옆에 걸어가던 친구가 보이지 않는다.

나는 친구를 여러 번 부른다.
들려오는 소리는 나뭇가지를 스치는
바람소리뿐.

아침 해는 어김없이 찾아오지만
함께 가던 친구가 보이지 않는다.
이 황당한 일이 또 어디 있나.
나는 친구를 잘 보살피지 못했을까?

산꼭대기에 먼저 올라간 이들과
언젠가 다시 만나면
무엇이라 말해야 하나.

AUTUMN NIGHT MOUNTAIN CLIMB

Autumn night after sunset,
A friend and I climb a mountain.

Cloud-covered, dim moonlight bears down heavily,
Branches brush against arms, legs, and faces.

How high have we come?
I don't see the friend who was walking beside me.

I call several times.
I hear only wind
Brushing through trees.

The morning sun comes without fail,
But I don't see my friend.
What an absurd situation.
Have I failed to look after him?

If I meet those
Who climbed ahead,
What should I say?

Translated from the Korean by Rachel S. Rhee

양을 위하여

내가 처음 키운 양들,
풀을 잘 뜯게 산에 방목했네.
밤이 되면 양들은 늑대들에게 쫓기고,
물어 뜯기고,
피를 흘리고,
내 분하고 아픈 마음
어떻게 할까?
늑대들을 쫓아다니며
한 마리도 남기지 않고 사냥해 버렸네.
정말 그것은 옳은 일이 아니었을까?
늑대들에게 쫓기지 않은
양들은 살만 쪄서
산기슭의 계곡溪谷에 넘어지면
죽음이 부를 때까지
다시는 일어날 수 없었네.
내 귀여운 양들.

FOR THE SHEEP

Sheep I rear for the first time,
turned out to pasture at the mountain.
Chased by wolves at night,
they are bitten
and they bleed.
What shall I do
with my vexed, distressed heart?
Chasing the wolves,
I hunted them, leaving not a single one.
Was that the right thing to do?
Sheep no longer chased by wolves
only grew fat,
and when they fell over within the gorge at the mountain's base,
could not rise again.
until death called.

Translated from the Korean by Rachel S. Rhee

펭귄

아무것도 먹지 않고
2달 만에 알을 깐
수컷 펭귄을 본다.

사랑이
무엇인지 보여준 펭귄,
매서운 눈보라도
아랑곳 않는 펭귄.

이제부터
나도 변해가리.
펭귄처럼 입 다물고
아무 불평도 하지 않겠다.

펭귄이 참아낸 사랑이
내게 기쁨이 되고
행복한 마음을 만들 줄이야.

PENGUIN

I look at the male penguin
that hatches an egg in two months
while eating nothing.

The penguin
demonstrating love,
the penguin disregarding
even fierce snowstorms.

From now on,
I shall also change.
Like a penguin, closing my mouth
and uttering no complaints.

That a love endured by the penguin
could become my joy
and catalyze a happy heart.

Translated from the Korean by Rachel S. Rhee

인생

누구나 들어보지 않았을 새 소리에
사람들은
가던 길을 멈추어 선다.

가게 앞에 놓인
새장 안에
한 마리 휘파람새가 앉아 있었다.

"새장에 갇혀 답답해서
구슬프게 운다!"고 말하는 이도 있었고
"즐겁게 노래한다!"고 말하기도 하였다.

그 새는 슬피 운다는 것을
보이지 않기라도 하려는 듯
또 한 번 즐겁게 휘파람을 분다.

LIFE

At the sound of a bird
nobody had heard before,
people halt their steps.

In a cage
in front of a shop,
sat a bush warbler:

"It's crying sadly because
it's trapped in a cage," said some;
"It sings joyfully!" said others.

As if trying not to show
that it was crying sadly,
it now joyfully whistles.

A songbird seen only in the spring or summer in Asia whose call sounds like whistling

Translated from the Korean by Rachel S. Rhee

나눔

산이나 들이나 집안이나
어디든 피어서
아름다움을 나누는 꽃을 보네.

잘 먹고 살찌워서
고기를 나누는
소와 돼지, 닭들.

가을엔
한 해 동안 잘 익혀온
열매 나누는 나무.

겨울엔
눈 속에 발을 묻고도
나뭇가지에 새의 둥지를 품어 주는 나무를 보네.

SHARING

Flowers bloom and share their beauty
no matter where—
in the mountains, in the fields, even inside a house.

And what about the cows, pigs, and chickens,
all who feed and fatten themselves
to sacrifice their flesh for us?

I see trees in the fall
sharing their fruit
that they have ripened all year long.

In winter, trees stand, their feet
buried deep in the snow, their branches
still hugging their bird nests.

Translated from the Korean by Kyung-Nyun Kim Richards & Steffen F. Richards

눈 내리는 날

아메리카의 북쪽에서
새들은 날아가고
희뿌연 구름 사이로
눈 폭풍은 나뭇가지를 흔들고 있다.
아이들이 눈뭉치로
대 조각가가 되어
눈사람을 만드니
초라한 내 모습을 보는 것만 같다.
이 겨울을 이기려면
여기저기 서 있는
눈사람 되어
독하게 살아야지.
눈 폭풍도 이제는 두렵지 않네.
아름다운 희망 앞에서는
사나운 겨울 눈보라도
나는 우습게 생각하네.

SNOWY DAY

In North America, birds soar
through hazy white clouds,
branches shake in a blizzard.
With snow, children transform
into great sculptors,
creating snowmen,
the image of my shabby self.
To triumph over the winter,
I will transform
into snowmen standing here and there,
and live strongly.
I don't fear blizzards anymore.
Even fierce winter snowstorms
are nothing to me
in the face of beautiful hope.

Translated from the Korean by Rachel S. Rhee

치와와

치와와는 개만 보았다 하면
마구 짖어대며
공격적이다,

집안에 있을 때는
너무도 평안하고
불평하지 않는다.

내가 외출했다가
집에 돌아오면
문 앞에서 깡충깡충 뛰기도 한다.

정치인들은 우리 치와와를 많이 닮았다.
개만 보았다 하면 마구 짖어대며
필사적으로 공격하니까.

CHIHUAHUA

When the chihuahua sees a dog,
it barks wildly
and is aggressive,

Inside
it's peaceful
and doesn't complain.

When I return home
after going out,
it jumps up and down at the door.

Politicians resemble my chihuahua.
Whenever they see a dog they bark wildly
and attack like it's life or death.

Translated from the Korean by Rachel S. Rhee

제 2부

Part Two

나무의 생각

먼 곳에서 나무를 바라보면
언제나 꼭 같은 숲으로 느껴진다.

그러나 가까이 와서 보면
나무는 모두 꼭 같지가 않다.

사람들만이 서로 다른 나무를
꼭 같은 나무로 만들려는 데는
큰 음모가 있다.

나무는 나무끼리 키도 다르고
잎사귀도 다르고
색깔도 다르다는 것을
나무는 서로서로 인정하고 있다.

유독 사람들만이
서로의 다름을
잘 인정하려 하지 않는다.

THE THOUGHTS OF TREES

Gazed at from afar,
Trees all seem like the same forest.

But observed up close,
Trees are not all the same.

There is a big conspiracy
In which only humans try to make
Different trees the same.

Trees mutually acknowledge
That each tree differs by height
Differs by leaf
And differs by color.

Only humans
Do not easily acknowledge
Each other's differences.

Translated from the Korean by Rachel S. Rhee

꽃나무

옮긴 뿌리는 하루에도 몇 번씩
일어섰다가 넘어지지만
꽃나무는 포기할 줄 모른다.

어둠뿐인 땅 속에서
어느 봄날 흙을 헤집고 나와
세상에서 한 번 웃어보기 위해서는

비를 맞아도
슬퍼하지 않는다.
비맞지 않고
크는 꽃나무가 있을까?

눈을 맞아도
마음마저 얼지 않는다.
눈 맞지 않고
겨울을 보내는 꽃나무가 있을까?

A BLOOMING TREE

Transplanted roots stand up and fall down
several times a day
but the blooming tree does not give up.

To dig itself out of the darkness of the soil
one spring day,
to be able to laugh in the world,

it does not grieve when the rain
strikes it.
What trees grow
without getting struck by the rain?

Even in the snow
its heart does not freeze.
What trees weather the winter
without snow falling on them?

Translation from the Korean by Kyung-Nyun Richards

장미의 힘으로

봄바람이 날 유혹하면
사랑의 눈빛으로 내 눈을 보세요.
파도가 물거품을 밀고 가듯이
내 영혼을 일깨워
당신이 지어놓은 집으로 데려가 주세요.

내 꿈속에서도 봄바람 불면
지친 눈빛으로 내 마음 문을 두드리세요.
향기가 사랑을 불태우듯이
장미의 힘으로
내 마음 문을 꼭 걸어 잠그세요.

WITH THE STRENGTH OF THE ROSE

When the spring wind entices me,
Please look at my eyes with the look of love.
Like waves carrying the foam along,
Awaken my spirit
And take me to the home that you built.

When the spring wind blows even in my dreams,
Knock at my heart's door with a weary regard.
Just as fragrance sets love aflame,
Lock my heart's door securely
With the strength of the rose.

Translated from the Korean by Rachel S. Rhee

다 뽑지 못한 가시 하나

장미의 입술에 취하면서도
나의 가시를 뽑는 것은 쉬운 일이 아니다.

파란 잎사귀로 장미를 감싸주지만
여전히 가시는 숨겨놓고 당신의 가슴을 찔러댄다.

장미는 나의 가시가 두려워도
언제나 모른 체 하네.

"사랑은 가시를 뽑는 것,
그것만이 행복을 줄 뿐이다."

가을바람은 장미 잎사귀를 다 떨어뜨리고
다 뽑았다고 믿은 나의 가시 하나를 보여주고 가네.

ONE THORN LEFT UNEXTRACTED

Even as I become drunk on the rose's lips,
pulling out my thorns is not easy.

Though with green leaves I enfold the rose,
I still hide my thorns and prick your chest.

The rose dreads the thorns
but always pretends not to know.

Love is what pulls out thorns,
Only that brings forth happiness.

The autumn wind blows off all the leaves
revealing one thorn left I thought extracted.

Translated from the Korean by Rachel S. Rhee

강

그대는 저쪽
나는 이쪽
그 사이에 강이 하나 있다.

너무 가까우면
정을 뗀다고

서로 마주 보고
그리워하라고

강은
우리를 갈라놓는가?
바다를 만나려면
강은 물을 버려야 하리

RIVER

You are there,
I am here
with a river between us.

Perhaps the river parts us,
because were we too close
we might hate each other.

So it leaves us apart,
to miss each other
from a distance.

Yet the river, too,
will surrender its water,
in order to meet the ocean.

Translated from the Korean by Irene S. Yoon

어디 이런 나무가 없을까?

가진 것 있다고 우쭐대지 않고
우뚝 서서 인생을 멀리 볼 줄 아는
키 큰 나무.

낮고 낮아져서
세상에 굽힐 줄 아는
작은 나무.

냇물처럼 느긋하고
부드럽게 가지 흔들며
거센 바람에도 꺾이지 않는
사랑의 나무.

하루를 살아도
늘 기쁘게 살아가는
행복한 나무.

세상에 어디
이런 나무가 없을까?

NO SUCH TREE ANYWHERE?

Not puffed up with possessions,
standing aloft and looking at a life far away,
a tree, a tall tree you are.

Shorter and shorter in height
making a bow to the world,
such a small tree you are.

Refreshed like water from a creek
tenderly waving its branches,
even a fierce wind cannot snap them off.

At the end of a day
always pleased to stand there,
a blissful tree.

Is there any such tree
in this world?

Translated from the Korean by Irene S. Yoon

가을의 시

가을 단풍이 들자
산에 서 있는 나무들이
몸살을 앓는다.

가을은 점점 깊어가고
바람은 나에게
더욱 차갑게 불어온다.

가을에 한 번씩
죽음을 연습하는 나무들,
나뭇잎들은 떨어져야한다.

겨울바람
세차게 불어오는 날에도
나무들은 견디어 내리라.

봄이 되면 어디서
그 많은 잎사귀가 돋아나고
더 성숙한 나무가 되리라.

POEM OF AUTUMN

When leaves change to autumn
standing trees in the mountain
become ill with fatigue.

Autumn gradually deepens
and the wind blows at me
ever more coldly.

Trees that practice death
once each autumn—
their leaves need to fall.

Even on days
when the winter wind gusts,
trees will endure.

When it's spring, from somewhere,
those many leaves will sprout
and it will become a more mature tree.

Translated from the Korean by Rachel S. Rhee

아들과 어머니

어머니, 먼 길을 가는데 무엇을 가지고 갈까요?
나는 아직도 기쁨을 가지고
남은 길을 가고 있지만
한 번도 나를 실망시키진 않았단다.
한 때는 나도 기쁨을 버리고
보석을 가지고 걸었지만
언제나 내 뼈를 말렸거든.
마음 속에 오래 지니고 다녀도
싫증나지 않는 것은 말이다.
기쁨은 빛의 선물이란다.
개구리가 슬픈 일을 전해도
한 발짝도 물러서지 말고
마음 속에서 기쁨의 친구를 꺼내 들어라.
인생길이란 그렇게 호락호락하지가 않단다.
그러니 아들아, 저 나뭇가지에 앉아
노래하는 새처럼 날마다 노래해 보렴.
"사랑합니다."
"감사합니다."

SON AND MOTHER

—Mother, what should I take on my long journey?
—Well, I'm still traveling on what's left
of the road with Joy,
but I've never been disappointed.
Once, I too threw Joy away
and proceeded with Jewel,
but it only sapped my bones.
You see, the thing you don't weary of,
even if carried a long time,
is Joy, a gift of the light.
Don't retreat a step
even when frogs deliver sad news,
but take out and hold
the friend of happiness
from within.
Well, life isn't that easy.
So, Son, sing every day
like birds sitting on those branches:
"I love you."
"Thank you."

Translated from the Korean by Rachel S. Rhee

질경이

아무리 감추어도
소용없네.
멀리 떨어져 있어도
어느 틈엔가 내 마음 속에
푸르게 돋아나는 질경이.
그냥 보는 것만으로도
가슴이 터져
견딜 수 없는 행복.
그대를 처음 만나던 날
그대는 이미 나의 질경이었네.
눈 감아도
그대는 나의 질경이.
질경이 꽃 하얗게
피우려 하네.
캘리포니아 사막에서
슬픔과 아픔의 눈물로
막으려 해도 소용없네.

PLANTAIN

All my concealing
is useless.
Even when far apart,
somehow budding greenly
in my heart, the plantain.
Even though far away,
a happiness I can't bear,
bursting now my heart.
You, when we first met,
became my plantain.
You, with eyes closed,
are still my plantain.
The plantain flower
is about to blossom in white.
In the California desert,
though I try to stop with tears
of sadness and pain,
it's useless.

Translated from the Korean by Rachel S. Rhee

세 발자국

한 가정의 꽃밭에서
한 발자국 가까이 있으면
장미꽃이라도 그 아름다움이 보이지 않네.

좀 더 멀리 서서
진정으로 바라보아도
꽃은 선명하게 보이지 않네.

세 발자국 떨어져서
신성한 눈빛으로 그대를 보면
내 마음속의 눈빛은 환하게 밝아지네.

내가 뱉은 말의 칼날에
줄줄 피 흘리는 그대 마음속의 상처도
더 분명하게 나타나네.

인생에도 세 발자국 떨어져서
서로를 볼 수 있다면
우리 서로 손잡고 갈 수 있을 것을.

THREE STEPS

In a family's garden
one step away is too close
to see the beauty of a rose.

A little farther away,
even a genuine gaze
still cannot see the flower vividly.

Three steps away,
seeing from a distance,
my heart-sight is clear.

I now clearly see
your bleeding wounds
by the dagger of my words.

If only we behold each other
three steps apart,
we could move on
hand in hand.

Translated from the Korean by Irene S. Yoon

한 마리 새

나는 잠시 겨울 숲길을 걸었다.
태평양 바다 건너
날아온
한 마리 새의 행복을 보려고.

나뭇잎이 다 떨어져 버린
회색빛 나뭇가지에 앉아서
새가 찾는 것이 무엇일까를 생각했다.

이렇게 넓고 넓은 새 땅에는
먹을 것이 많아도 소용없네.

눈을 감고 있는 새는
오늘 밤
홀로 잠들지 못하네.

ONE BIRD

I walked a winter forest path awhile
to see the happiness of a bird
which flew
across the Pacific.

I pondered what the bird was seeking,
sitting on gray branches
from which leaves had already fallen.

In this vast new country,
so much to eat yet how useless.

The bird with closed eyes
cannot fall asleep alone
tonight.

Translated from the Korean by Rachel S. Rhee

나비

나비 한 마리에게
사랑한다는 말은 왜 할 수 없을까?
사랑하니까.

가끔은 흥분해서
내가 헤어지자고 말할까?
헤어지기 싫어서.

때로는 나비가
날아가 버리라고 손뼉을 친다.
함께 있고 싶어서.

나비 한 마리가 내 침상에
펄럭펄럭 날아 와서 기쁨을 주듯이
나 또한 그대 위해 꽃을 피우리.

BUTTERFLY

Why am I unable to speak of love
to one butterfly?
Because I love.

Should I become agitated at times
and suggest we should separate?
Because I do not want to part.

Sometimes I clap
so the butterfly will fly away.
Because I want to be together.

Just as one butterfly fluttering over
to my bed gives joy,
I too shall bloom a flower for you.

Translated from the Korean by Rachel S. Rhee

갈대

갈대는 울지 않는다.
바람이 울고 갈뿐

하늘엔 천둥과 번개가 울고 가지만
그것도 잠시 후면 지나간다.

갈대는 언제나
살이 찌면 죽는다는 것을 안다.

오랜 고통의 세월
상한 마음도 기쁨으로 이겨낸 그대.

누가 이 갈대를
운다고 말하는가?

인고의 세월이 지난 어느 가을날
갈대는 하얀 꽃 하나 피워냈다.

REED

The reed does not weep,
Only the wind weeps then departs.

In the sky, thunder and lightning cry
Yet, after a moment, they too pass.

The reed always knows
That weight gain is death.

You who conquered with joy a bruised heart,
A long period of suffering.

Who would say
This reed weeps?

One autumn day when the season of endurance had passed,
The reed brought forth a white blossom.

Translated from the Korean by Rachel S. Rhee

나무처럼

나무처럼
내가
살아야 하리

한없이
낮고 낮아져서
물을 빨아올리는 나무가 되고

가을볕에 익혀온
열매 주고도
기뻐하는 나무처럼

가을바람에
가진 잎을 모두 내려놓고도
대지를 품어주는 나무가 되고

하늘을 우러러
두 손 들고 기도하면서도
새가 되려고 하지 않는 나무처럼

LIKE A TREE

I
shall live
like a tree

I'll become a tree
that siphons water
from ever lowering

like a tree that rejoices
despite giving its fruit
ripened in the autumn sun

and become a tree that embraces earth
despite laying down
all its leaves in the autumn wind

like a tree that doesn't try to be a bird
even as it lifts up its boughs to pray
its face turned to the sky

Translated from the Korean by Rachel S. Rhee

큰 나무 한 그루

아무나 결코 할 수 없네.
큰 나무가 해낸 일.

해마다 이웃들에게
가을 잎사귀를 내어주는 일.

무더운 여름날에는 나무 밑에 앉아
힘겨운 삶을 쉬어가게 그늘을 주는 일.

차가운 겨울날에는 밤을 지새울 새를
나뭇가지마다 품어주는 일.

큰 나무는 이처럼 멀리 바라보지만
나는 고작해야 큰 나무나 쳐다보네.

ONE BIG TREE

It's not something anyone can do,
what the big tree accomplished.

Giving autumn leaves
to neighbors each year.

Providing shade for those sitting beneath it
to rest from a hard life on hot summer days.

Embracing birds spending the night
on its branches during cold winter days.

In this way, the big tree gazes great-heartedly afar
but I at most can only look at the big tree.

Translated from the Korean by Rachel S. Rhee

작은 꽃씨 하나

작은 꽃씨 하나
땅에 떨어져
아름다운 꽃을 피우네.

작은 사랑 하나
마음에 심어
가정을 낙원으로 만드네.

작은 기쁨 하나
사람들에게 심어
하늘나라 문을 열게 하네.

당신도 심어보렴.
작은 것이라도
때가 되면 심은 대로 거두리니.

ONE SMALL FLOWER SEED

One small flower seed
fallen on the ground
blooms into a beautiful blossom.

One small love
planted in the heart
turns a home into paradise.

One small joy
planted within people
makes Heaven's gates open.

You try planting, too.
Even if it's something small
when it's time, you'll reap as you've sown.

Translated from the Korean by Rachel S. Rhee

기차

먹이를 찾아 헤매던
한 때의 새들을 싣고
기차는 떠났다.

간이역은 잠시 적막에 쌓였다.
기차가 다시 오지 않아
철길은 녹슨 채 뻗어 있다.

이 지루한 겨울이 가면
또다시 봄은 오고
이마에 걸려 있던 구름도 떠나가리라.

다시 새들이 찾아올
기차를 나는 기다린다.

벌판도 흔들고
철길도 반짝이는 그 날이 오면
나도 평안을 찾으리라.

TRAIN

The train left
carrying birds
which used to wander for food.

The small train stop is covered in solitude,
tracks stretching out in a rusted state
because the train did not return.

When this tedious winter passes,
spring will come again and clouds
which had hung on my forehead will leave.

I wait for the train
which birds will again seek.

When that day comes,
when fields shake and tracks sparkle,
I, too, shall find peace.

Translated from the Korean by Rachel S. Rhee

마음

깨어지기 쉬운 것은
땅바닥에 떨어뜨린
질그릇이다.

깨어지기 쉬운 것은
초겨울 날
강바닥의 살얼음이다.

이보다도 더
깨어지기 쉬운 것은
말 한 마디에
그 상처 난 사람의 마음이다.

HEART

That which is easy to break
is earthenware
dropped on the floor.

That which is easy to break
is thin ice on the river's surface
on an early winter day.

That which is easy to break
even more than these
is the heart of a person
hurt easily by a single word.

Translated from the Korean by Rachel S. Rhee

눈의 비밀

사랑을 좋아하는 사람은
하늘의 햇빛만 본다.

미움을 좋아하는 사람은
땅의 어둠만 본다.

무엇을 보느냐에 따라
인생은 달라진다.

THE SECRET OF EYES

He who likes love
looks only at sunlight in the sky.

He who likes hatred
looks only at the land's darkness.

Depending on what you look at,
life changes.

Translated from the Korean by Rachel S. Rhee

사랑 가꾸기

방안에 있는
snake-plant에
자주 물을 주었다.

어느 날 잎사귀가
육중한 무게를 견디지 못해
툭! 떨어진다.

물이 완전히 마를 때까지
시간을 두고 기다려야지.
snake-plant를 살리기 위해서는

너무 세심하게 챙겨주지 말아야지.
지나치게 보살펴 주지도 말아야지.
우리가 사랑하는 것들을 살리기 위해서는

CULTIVATING LOVE

I frequently watered
the snake plant
in the room.

One day, leaves
swish! fell
unable to bear the heavy weight.

I shall wait until
the water dries completely
to save the snake plant.

I won't look after it prudently
I won't take care of it too zealously
to save the things we love.

Translated from the Korean by Rachel S. Rhee

하얀 민들레

민들레처럼 살아야 하리.

민들레는 울부짖었네.
물은 점점 불어
모가지까지 차오르는데

뿌리는 깊어 빠지지 않고
얼마나 안간힘 썼으면
머리카락마저도 백발이 되었을까.

길거리의 시멘트 갈라진 틈이나
양지바른 언덕배기 그 어디든 심어주어
노란 꽃을 피우게 하신 당신.

영원히 살고 싶어
나는 죽고 가벼워져서
당신을 닮았지

그 은혜가 고마워서 세상 끝까지
당신의 말씀 하얗게 머리에 이고
바람에 날개를 달았지.

WHITE DANDELION

I need to live like the dandelion.

The dandelion cried out,
water gradually swelling
up to its neck

but deep roots refuse to be pulled out.
So strenuously did it strain
that even its hair turned white.

You cause yellow flowers to bloom,
planting seeds everywhere, on sunny hilltops
or in cement cracks in the street.

Wanting to live forever,
I died and became lighter
and so became like You.

Thankful for that grace, I carried Your words
whitely on my head to the ends of the earth
with wings hung by the wind.

Translated from the Korean by Rachel S. Rhee

눈과 죄

거친 겨울 들판에 쏟아지는
부드럽고 하얀 눈.

소리 없이 내리는 눈이
내 가슴에서 찾는 것은
포도주같이 붉은 죄

두꺼운 겨울 외투로 눈을 피해 보지만
눈은 내리고 또 내린다.

밤새워 어둠 속에서 눈과 싸우다가
나는 기쁨을 찾았다.

아침에 일어나니 하얀 눈 위에
내 죄가 피를 흘렸네

SNOW AND SIN

Soft, white snow
Falling on the rough winter field.

What snow falling without sound
Looks for within my heart
Is sin as red as wine.

With a thick winter coat, I try to avoid the snow,
But it keeps falling and falling.

While fighting with snow all night in darkness,
I found happiness.

When I woke in the morning,
My sin had shed blood on the white snow.

Translated from the Korean by Rachel S. Rhee

어머니의 사랑

내가 어릴 때 넘어져도
어머니는 스스로 일어나게
나를 일으켜 세워주지 않으셨다.

내가 찬사를 받고 싶을 때에도
어머니는 재능을 더 쌓으라고
위인들의 얘기를 들려주셨지.

내가 행복하기를 바랐을 때에도
어머니는 깨우치게
마음이 늘 기뻐하며 살라고 타일러주셨다.

내가 기대고 싶을 때에도
어머니는 남이 기대는 어깨가 되라고
과분한 책임감을 주셨지.

MOTHER'S LOVE

When I fell as a child
Mother did not help me stand
So that I would rise by myself.

When I wanted to receive praise
Mother recounted stories of great men
So that I would develop my gifts.

When I felt depressed
Mother advised me to live with joy
So that I would be enlightened.

When I wanted to lean on others
Mother told me to be a shoulder on which others could lean
Giving me a large sense of responsibility.

Translated from the Korean by Rachel S. Rhee

그대와 나

그대와 나
함께 가는 먼 길에
가을바람이 불면
나는 마음에 단풍이 든다.
한 번 불어온 가을바람은
자꾸자꾸 흔들다보니
마음의 작은 상처들도
큰 상처가 되어
사랑의 마음들마저
우수수 낙엽이 되어 떨어지네.
그렇지, 그대가 가는 곳마다
그리고 우리가 함께 달려 가야할 곳에
나는 봄바람의 새 옷을 입고
일생동안 기쁜 노래 불러주고
사랑한다고 말하며
달려가야 하네.

YOU AND I

You and I
when travelling together on the long road
the autumn wind blows,
my heart takes on autumnal tints.
The autumn wind which blew in
keeps agitating on and on until
even small heart wounds
become large wounds
so that even the hearts of love
become autumn leaves and *whoosh* fall.
That's right, everywhere you go
and where we are to run together,
I shall run
wearing new clothes of the spring wind
singing joyful songs for life
and speaking of love.

Translated from the Korean by Rachel S. Rhee

사과나무의 사랑

그해 봄,
뒤뜰에 사과나무 두 그루 심었다.

가을이 되니
한 그루 사과나무에는
사과가 많이 달렸다.

새들이 사과나무 위에
모이는 이유를 알겠다.
사과향기를 물씬 풍겨주었다.

나는 다른 사과나무에게도 갔는데
사과 한 개도 열리지 않았다.

새들도 외면하고 있었다.
사과 향기 대신 외로움과 질투심이
나를 노려보았다.

THE LOVE OF AN APPLE TREE

Spring that year,
I planted two apple trees in the back yard.

When it became autumn,
on one tree
hung many apples.

I think I know why
birds gather on top of that tree.
It strongly gave off an apple bouquet.

I went to the other apple tree
but it had not a single apple.

Birds also avoided it.
In lieu of apple perfume,
loneliness and jealousy glared at me.

Translated from the Korean by Rachel S. Rhee

하늘의 꽃

햇빛만이 가득한 하늘
그 속에서 탐스럽게 피어 있는 꽃.

내 마음이 이끌리어 꺾었다.
그 작은 꽃 하나.

하지만 이 꽃이 뭐길래
까마귀는 날마다 내 심장을 쪼고 있을까?

그 꽃 하나 꺾기 위해
시인들은 또 도토리 죽도 마다하지 않는 것일까?

그 비밀은 아무도 모른다.
마음이 이끌리는 하늘의 꽃.

HEAVEN'S FLOWER

A tempting flower in bloom
in the sky full of only sunlight.

It tugged at my heart so I plucked it,
that single small blossom.

But what is this flower
that a raven pecks my heart daily?

Why, to pick that flower,
do poets not spurn even the porridge of poverty?

Nobody knows that secret.
Flower of heaven which lures my heart.

Translated from the Korean by Rachel S. Rhee

조윤호 시집 서평

조윤호 시인의 시는 섬세하고, 세세하며, 독자들을 예민한 아름다움으로 감동시킨다. 책의 제일 첫 번째 시 "사과나무"는 그 자체로서 한국시의 훌륭한 특징을 잘 보여 주는데— 적어도 이 독자가 보기에는— 그것은 마치 초점을 맞추어 관찰하는 예술가의 눈 같으며, 독자들을 흠칫 멈추게 하는 정직함의 접근 가능성, 우물 속의 반짝이는 거울처럼 깊은 심오함을 나타낸다.

조윤호 시인의 자연에 대한 경외심과 그의 창작적 비전의 절제 있는 간결함을 나는 사랑한다.

—피터 태빗 죤스

영국 웨일즈 시인/ 발행인

딜란 토마스의 딸, 애런위 토마스와 함께 공저로 *딜란 토마스의 뉴욕 그레니치 빌리지 탐방*이 있음. 시집 The Lizard Catcher 외 다수.

COMMENTS ON POETRY BOOK
BY YOON-HO CHO

The poems of Yoon-Ho Cho are delicate, detailed, and strike the reader with their sensitive beauty. The opening poem , *Apple Tree*, illustrates in itself the wonderful qualities of Korean poetry, which— for me at least— are an artist's eye for focused observation, an arresting and honest accessibility, and depths as deep as the shining mirror of a well.

I love Yoon-Ho Cho's poet's veneration of nature and the controlled conciseness of his creative vision.

—Peter Thabit Jones

Welsh poet and publisher

Author (with Aeronwy Thomas, daughter of Dylan Thomas)

of the *Dylan Thomas Walking Tour of Greenwich Village*

　조윤호 시인의 영적 제분소의 나락에서는 한겨울 얼음의 유리에서 잘라낸 지혜가 나온다, 마치 잘 깎여진 금강석이 다수의 측면으로 구성된 프리즘으로 자연의 심오한 진실을 들어내듯이—그들의 순결함은 자양이 되고, 깊은 소박함은 감탄을 자아낸다. 조 시인의 시를 체험하는 것은 에로스와 손을 잡고, 변형을 위한 우리의 내재적 욕구의 여정을 따르는 것이다. 고맙습니다, 조 시인님, 이 훌륭한 시선집을 내주셔서. 이제 그 시들은 저의 생명의 나무에 새로운 에메랄드 가지를 돋아나게 했습니다.

—캐롤린 메리 클리펠드

미국시인, 화가
*Psyche of Mirrors*이다. *A Promenade of Portraits,*
〈방랑의 새벽〉 〈영혼의 씨앗〉 외 다수의 시집이 있다.

From the grist of Yoon-Ho Cho's spiritual mill come wisdoms spliced from the glass of winter's ice, like finely cut diamonds revealing their multi-faceted prisms of Nature's deeper truths—nourishing in their innocence, awesome in their profound simplicity. As we experience Mr. Cho's poetry, we journey hand in hand with Eros in our innate need to transform. Thank you, Mr. Cho, for this grand selection of poems, for they have sprouted a new emerald limb on my tree of life.

—Carolyn Mary Kleefeld

Poet, Artist, Author of *Vagabond Dawns, Soul Seeds,*
Psyche of Mirrors: A Promenade of Portraits

시 「갈대」를 읽고

이 형 권

문학평론가/ 충남대 교수

이 시에서 "갈대"는 가냘픈 외모 때문에 흔히 연약한 존재를 비유하는데 많이 활용하는 소재이다. 그러나 이 시에서의 "갈대"는 사정이 다르다.

시의 서두를 "갈대는 울지 않는다"로 시작하는 것만 보아도 "갈대"는 연약한 존재가 아니다. 오히려 "바람"이나 "천둥 번개"와 같이 잠시 지나가고 마는 것들보다 강한 존재이다. 그래서 "갈대"는 "살이 찌면 죽는다"는 것을 각성하고 사는 절제된 삶의 상징이며 "오랜 고통의 세월"도 "기쁨으로 이겨낸" 강인한 존재이다. 그러므로 「갈대」를 운다고 표현하는 것이 잘못이라고 하는 시인의 주장은 시적 설득력이 충분하다.

울음이란 자아의 연약성이 겉으로 드러난 징표라고 한다면, 시련을 극복한 「갈대」는 강인한 생명력을 상징한다.

온갖 고통이나 시련을 이겨낸 자의 모습은 언제나 아름답다. "어느 가을날"에 "하얀 꽃을 피워"낸 "갈대"가 바로 그런 모습이다. 이 시는 무엇보다도 "갈대"에 대한 시적 해석이 신선하다는 점에서 주목할 만하다.

이 시의 "갈대"는 파스칼이 인간을 '생각하는 갈대'라고 하여 인간의 사유 능력을 강조하고, 신경림이 '저 혼자 조용히 우는 갈대'라고 하여 실존으로 연약한 인간상을 상징한 것과 다르다. 사실 좋은 시의 요건 가운데 핵심적인 것 하나는 인식의 새로움이다. 이 시는 그런 새로움을 확보했다.

On the "Reed"

—Hyung Kwon Lee

Literary Critic / Chung Nam U. Professor

The reed is a subject matter commonly used as a metaphor for frailty due to its fragile outward appearance. However, the reed in this poem is different.

Even the beginning which states "The reed does not cry" shows that the reed is not fragile. Instead, it is stronger than even things which pass briefly like "the wind" or "thunder and lightning." Hence, the reed symbolizes the life of moderation which recognizes that "weight gain is death" and it is a strong existence which "won out with joy". . ."the long time of suffering." Therefore, Cho's argument—that a portrayal of a crying reed is incorrect—sufficiently convinces.

If tears are the external expression of the self's frailty, the reed which conquered suffering symbolizes the tough will to live.

The image of one who has conquered all kinds of suffering and difficulties is always beautiful. That is the image of the "reed" which "brought forth a white blossom". . ."one autumn day." This poem is worth scrutinizing, for more than anything, the freshness of its poetic interpretation of the "reed."

Cho's view of the reed differs from both Pascal's view, which emphasized man's ability to reason, calling humans the "thinking reed," as well as from Kyung Rim Shin's view, which symbolized the fragile existence of mankind with "The Reed That Cries Alone." In fact, the core of the necessary requisites of a good poem is new perception. This poem has secured that kind of newness.

시 「우리가 꽃이 되어 준다면」을 읽고

송 기 한

시인/ 대전대 교수

너무도 흔한 말 같지만 '사랑'이 지닌 에너지에 관한 한 우리가 아무리 강조해도 지나치지 않다. 너무도 쉽게 오가는 말이어서 신선함도 생명력도 모두 바래지고 관성화 되어 버린 말이지만 실제로 '사랑'이 없이 살아갈 수 있는 존재는 아무도 없다. 모든 생명체가 그러한데 하물며 인간의 경우 예외가 뭘까? 시인의 시에는 '사랑'이 가득하다. 사실 대상을 그윽이 바라보는 '사랑'의 시선 없이 시는 쓰여 지지 않는다. 대상을 감싸는 따뜻한 마음이 없이는 결코 창조적이지 못하다.

다시 말해 모든 시는 사랑의 마음에 의해 탄생한다. 그러한데도 유독 시인의 시들에 '사랑'이 가득함이 느껴지는 이유는 무엇일까? 무엇보다 그의 시에는 '실천'이 있다. 사랑을 위한, 사랑을 나누기 위한 구체적인 행위와 실천적인 행동이 있는 것이다.

시인은 누군가 나에게 사랑을 '주기'를 기다리지 않는다. 남이 나에게 다가와, 나에게 베풀고 나를 배려해 주기를 바라지 않는다.

그는 기다리는 대신 그가 먼저 나서고 그가 직접 행한다. 그는 자신이 직접 섬기고 스스로 남을 배려한다. 시인은 우리에게 우리가 먼저 무엇이 '되라'고 제안한다. '꽃이 되'라고. '길'이 되'라고 말한다. '따뜻한 마음을 주'라고, '둘이 하나 되어 주'라고 말한다. '사랑'은 멀리 있는 것이 아니라 작은 것 하나에서부터, 작은 일 하나하나에 대해 항상 긍정하고 기뻐하는 마음 속에서 피어나는 것이리라.

남을 위해 먼저 내가 행동하는 데서부터 시작되는 것이리라. 이 점을 실천하는 시인의 시에는 긍정에서 비롯되는 강한 온기의 에너지가 흐른다.

On "If We Became Flowers"

—By Ki Han Song

Poet/ Dae Jeon U. Professor

No matter how much emphasis we place on the energy of "love," which seems oft spoken, we would still fail to overdo it. "Love" is something so easily said that freshness and power fade and become inert, yet nothing can live without it. When all living things are this way, how could humans be an exception? Cho's poem is filled with "love." In fact, without the gaze of "love" looking at its object, poems cannot be written. Without a warm heart enfolding its object, one can never be creative.

In other words, all poems are born through the heart of love. Then why is it that Cho's poems are especially filled with "love?" More than anything, his poems have "practice"— concrete behaviors and actions put into practice in order to share love.

Cho does not wait for someone to "give" him love. He does not wish for someone to approach him, to bestow upon him, to show solicitude towards him. Instead of waiting, he himself first steps forward and acts . He himself serves others and shows concern for others on his own. Cho suggests that we should "[become]" something first— to "[become] a flower," to "[become] pathways." He tells us to "[give] warm hearts," that "two [become] one." "Love" is not something far away but something that blossoms from each small thing as well as from the heart that affirms and rejoices in each and every small act.

Love begins from the place where I first act for others. Cho's poem, which puts this point into practice, has flowing through it the strong warmth of energy which begins in affirmation.

KOREAN TRANSLATORS

Rachel S. Rhee earned a B.A. in English Language and Literature from the University of Chicago and an M.A. in Counseling from Eastern University, PA. She immigrated from Korea at age six and has been translating Korean poetry for over ten years, ever since she received the Korean Expatriate Literature Magazine Translation Award in 2000. She currently works as a psychotherapist in Pennsylvania.

레이철 S. 리 : 6세 때 도미. 시카고 대학에서 영문학 학사, 이스턴 대학에서 카운슬링으로 석사 학위 취득. 2000년에 「해외문학」 지 신인상 번역부문상 수상 이후 주로 한국시를 영어로 번역해 왔으며, 현재 펜실베이니아에서 심리치료사로 일하고 있다.

Irene S. Yoon : Poet-Translator and staff editor of *Korean Expatriate Literature*. B.A in English Literature from Ewha Women's University in Korea, and earned an M.A. in TESOL from Fairleigh Dickinson University, NJ. She won the translation award with *Girls' Night Out* from Hewemunhak in 2008. She translates poems and short stories bilingually in Korean and English, contributing to Korean-American literary exchange. She lives in New Jersey.

윤선주 : 시인, 번역가. "해외문학" 편집위원. 이화여대 영문학과, 미국 Fairleigh Dickinson Univ. 대학원 졸업. 2008년 작가 안설희 씨의 단편소설 영역 『밤나들이』로 "해외문학" 신인상 번역부문에 당선되어 등단. 미국 시인 캐롤린 메리 클리펠드의 시집 "방랑의 새벽" (Vagabond Dawns)을 번역 출간(2012). 한인작가들과 미국인 작가들의 영시와 단편소설을 번역, "해외문학"지와 미국 현대시 잡지 등에

소개하며 한미문학 교류에 노력. 현재 뉴저지에 거주.

Kyung-Nyun Kim Richards is a poet, essayist, and translator of Korean literature. Korean born, she has lived in the US since 1967 and writes both in Korean and English. Her translations include *Dictée* (by Theresa H-K Cha), *Sky, Wind, and Stars* (by Yun Dong-Ju), and *The Love of Dunhuang* (by Yun Humyong). Her original work was collected in *Snail* (in Korean). A recipient of The Top Prize in Poetry Translation from The Korea Times Translation Contest (1996) and the 39th Translation Award from PEN Korea (2006). E-mail: richards kyungnyun@gmail.com

김경년: 서울에서 출생한 시인이며 수필가, 그리고 한영문학 번역가이다. 김 여류시인은 UC Berkeley대학교 교수, "해외문학" 편집위원 및 자문위원, 해외문인협회 회원인데 저서로 시집 "달팽이가 그어놓은 작은 점선"이 있다. 번역서로는 윤동주 시집 "별 헤는 밤", "Sky, Wind, and Stars", 김승희 시집 "I WANT TO HIJACK AN AIRPLANE" 등 다수. 1996년 The Korea Times 현대문학 번역상 (시부문), 2006년 한국 국제펜 문학상을 각각 수상한 바 있다.

Steffen Francis Richards : A native of San Francisco Bay Area, Steffen Francis Richards attended U.C. Berkeley receiving a B.A. in History and Oriental Languages and an M.A. in Oriental Languages (Japanese). He is a poet, essayist, and sometime translator of Japanese. Since 1996, he has co-translated Korean literature with his wife, Kyung-Nyun Kim Richards. His co-translations include *Sky, Wind, and Stars* by Yoon Dong-Ju (2003), *I Want to Hijack an Airplane* by Kim Seung-Hee (2004), *The Love of Dunhuang* by Yun Humyong (2005), *Memoirs of a Soldier* (Col. Kay In-Ju, unpublished manuscript, 2004), *Life Within an Egg* (Korean/English Bilingual Edition) by Kim Seung-Hee (2007).

His poems were published in *Light, Dark Wind, Moon*, Aventine Press

LLC (2004) and *The Seventh Quarry*; essays in *The New Oxford Review*; and translations in *Literature East & West* and *Journal of Concerned Asian Scholars*.

스테픈 프란시스 리챠즈는 샌프란시스코 베이지역에서 태어나 U.C. Berkeley에서 역사학과 동양어 전공으로 학사 학위와 석사학위 (일본 문학) 를 취득했다. 그는 시인, 수필가, 일본어번역가이다. 1996년부터 아내이자 한국문학 번역가 김경년과 함께 한국문학 공역자로 윤동주 시전집 *Sky, Wind, and Stars*, 김승희 시선집 *I Want to Hijack an Airplane*, 윤후명 소설 *The Love of Dunhuang*, 김승희 이중언어판 시선집 *Life Within an Egg* 등을 펴냈다.

그의 시는 *Light, Dark Wind, Moon* 과 *The Seventh Quarry* 등에 발표 되었으며, 수필은 *The New Oxford Review*에, 번역 작품은 *Literature East & West*와 *Journal of Concerned Asian Scholars* 등에 발표 되었다.

| 작가에 관하여 |

조윤호는 1938년 경상남도 창원에서 출생했다. 그는 동국대학교 문리대 물리학과를 졸업. 1964에서 1971년까지 동양방송(TBC 라디오 & TV) 기자로 활동했다.

그는 1963년 "자유문학" 신인상에 시가 당선되어 문단에 데뷔. 1971년 미국에 이민. 그의 작품들은 미국의 시전문지 *Lips, The Paterson Literary Review* 와 영국 웨일즈의 시 전문지 *The Seventh Quarry* 등에 시를 발표해 오고 있다. 저서로는 시집 4권을 출간했는데 1986년 첫 시집 《풀꽃처럼 만나리》에 이어 1992년 《시인 나무》와 1997년 《고뇌하는 당신》 2006년 《강은 마음을 비운다》를 출간했다.

그는 1997년 제4회 "가산문학상"을 수상한 데 이어 2012년에 "미주시인상"(미주시인협회)을 수상.

조윤호는 미국시인 스탠리 발칸(Stanley H. Barkan 미국 출판사 Cross-Cultural Communications 대표)과 공동 발행인 겸 편집인으로 국제 시집인 《한미 현대시》(BRIDGING THE WATERS=물 위에 다리놓기)를 2013년에 출간하기도 했다.

현재 그는 국제펜클럽 미국 본부 회원이며 미국에서 발행되는 "해외문학" 발행인 겸 편집인으로 활동하고 있다.

그는 "해외문인협회" 제 2대 회장을 역임했다. (2002-2005)

ABOUT THE AUTHOR

Yoon-Ho Cho was born in 1938 in South Korea. He graduated from Dong-Guk University with Bachelor's Degree in Physics. From 1964 to 1971, he was a news reporter for TBC radio and television in Seoul, South Korea.

Yoon-Ho Cho made his literary debut in 1963 by winning the New Writer's Award of the Korean journal *Jayu Munhak* (Freedom Literature). He immigrated to the US in 1971 and has published in the American poetry journals *Lips* and *The Paterson Literary Review,* as well as the Welsh poetry journal *The Seventh Quarry*. His four published books of poetry include his first published work, *Meet Like Wildflowers* (1985), *The Poet's Tree* (1992), *You, the Suffering Brooder* (1997), *The River Empties Its Heart* (2006).

He also co-published and co-edited the international anthology of poetry *Bridging the Waters* (2013) with Stanley H. Barkan (founder of the Cross-Cultural Communications publishing company).

His awards include the 4th annual Gasan Literature Award (1997), and, the Korean-American Poet Association's Literature Award (2012).

A member of PEN USA, Yoon-Ho Cho is the editor-publisher of the journal *Korean Expatriate Literature* (USA).

He was the second President of the Korean Expatriate Literary Association, 2002-2005.